All About Animals

An illustrated guide to creatures
great and small

ARCTURUS

ARCTURUS

This edition published in 2022 by
Arcturus Publishing Limited
26/27 Bickels Yard, 151–153 Bermondsey Street,
London SE1 3HA

Author: Polly Cheeseman
Illustrator: Iris Deppe
Designer: Stefan Holliland
Editor: Violet Peto
Consultant: Anne Rooney
Managing Editor: Joe Harris

ISBN: 978-1-3988-1115-7
CH010040NT
Supplier 29, Date 0622, PI 00002183

Printed in China

Contents

All the Animals 4

On the Hunt 6

Coral Reef 8

Family Life 10

Amazing Amphibians 12

The Life of a Frog 14

Make a Mini Wildlife Pond 16

African Grasslands 18

Gentle Giants 20

In the Freezer 22

Scaly Reptiles 24

Deep-Sea Hunters 26

Special Skills 28

Living Together 30

Life in the Desert 32

On the Move 34

Big Bouncers 36

Out in the Dark 38

Collect Animal Footprints 40

Venom and Poison 42

Friendly Dolphins 44

Animals in Danger 46

Glossary 48

All the Animals

From the bottom of the oceans to the skies above us, our planet is filled with millions of incredible creatures. We group animals by things that they have in common.

All birds have feathers and wings—though not all birds can fly. Birds lay eggs, which their chicks hatch from. They are warm-blooded, have bony skeletons, and breathe air.

Reptiles, such as snakes, lizards, and turtles, are cold-blooded, which means that they need to warm themselves in the sun. Their skin is tough and scaly. Most reptile babies hatch from eggs.

4

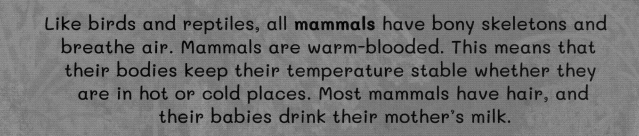

Like birds and reptiles, all **mammals** have bony skeletons and breathe air. Mammals are warm-blooded. This means that their bodies keep their temperature stable whether they are in hot or cold places. Most mammals have hair, and their babies drink their mother's milk.

People are mammals, too!

Amphibians, such as frogs and toads, begin life in water. As adults, most can also live on land. Their skin needs to be kept damp. They breathe with **gills**, lungs, or through their skin.

Invertebrates are creatures that do not have a skeleton inside their bodies. They include flying insects, soft-bodied worms, and sea creatures, such as crabs and sea anemones.

Fish live under water in rivers, lakes, and oceans. Their bodies are covered with scales, and they have fins to help them swim. They use their gills to take in **oxygen** from the water.

On the Hunt

Wolves are famous for their loud howl. Wolves are **predators**, which means they hunt other animals for food.

Wolves live in groups called packs. The pack is made up of a male and female leader, and their young. There can be as many as 30 wolves in a pack.

Moose

Wolves hunt in packs. They signal to each other and try and surround their **prey**. By working together, wolves can bring down large animals, such as moose and deer.

Wolves have large ears and excellent hearing. They can hear prey from far away. They are also able to hear the howls of other wolves.

With long, strong legs, wolves are able to sprint after fast-moving prey. Wolves travel long distances searching for food.

A wolf has powerful jaws and sharp teeth. This helps the wolf grip onto its prey.

Coral Reef

A **coral reef** is like an amazing underwater garden. Found in **tropical** seas, coral reefs provide food and shelter for thousands of bright and beautiful creatures.

Coral is made by a group of tiny creatures called polyps. The polyps build a hard bony home around themselves. Over many years, different corals join to form large reefs.

Groups of brightly-patterned fish dart in and out of the coral, looking for food. The reef is filled with handy places where fish can hide from **predators**.

Moorish idol

Finger coral

Sea slug

Reef sharks hunt for small fish in the warm, shallow waters.

Sea turtles come to the reef to feed on sea creatures such as jellyfish and sea sponges. Like other aquatic **reptiles**, turtles must swim to the surface to breathe air.

Butterfly fish

Sea sponge

9

Family Life

Elephants are the largest land animal. Even though they are strong and powerful, these **mammals** are gentle giants. Elephants look after their young for longer than any other animal—apart from humans.

Elephants live in family groups. Families can join together to form larger **herds**. The oldest female is the leader. She helps the others find water and watches over them when they rest.

A female elephant carries her baby inside her for nearly two years before it is born. This is longer than any other mammal. A baby elephant is called a calf.

When a calf is born, the mother uses her trunk to help it stand and drink her milk. The calf can walk soon after it's born. The calf stays with its mother for up to 10 years.

Mother

Calf

Other elephants in the herd help look after the young. They protect calves from **predators**. By watching their elders, calves learn to use their trunks to pick grass and leaves to eat.

Amazing Amphibians

Frogs, toads, and salamanders all belong to a group of animals called **amphibians**. As adults, most amphibians are able to live on land and in the water.

Amphibians are cold-blooded, which means that they cannot control their body temperature. They become warmer or cooler depending on their surroundings.

Even though most amphibians have lungs to breathe, they take in most of their **oxygen** through their skin. Their smooth skin needs to be kept damp, so they stay close to water.

Salamanders look a bit like lizards. Most are small, but the Chinese giant salamander is the largest in the world. It can grow longer than the height of a man!

Some amphibians have bright or patterned skin. This is a warning for **predators** not to attack them. Their skin can taste nasty and even contain poison!

Frogs have very long and strong back legs. They use them to leap on land and to swim under water. Tree frogs have sticky pads on their feet to help them climb.

Red-eyed tree frog

Sticky pads

Strong back legs

Toads may look like frogs, but usually they are larger and spend more time on land than frogs do. Their skin looks dry and bumpy. Some toads croak very loudly.

The Life of a Frog

Most amphibians start life looking very different to how they look as adults. A frog's body goes through big changes as it grows. This is called **metamorphosis**.

First, the female frog lays a big blob of eggs in water. She can lay more than a thousand eggs. The eggs are called frogspawn. Each egg has a jellylike layer around a dark spot.

1

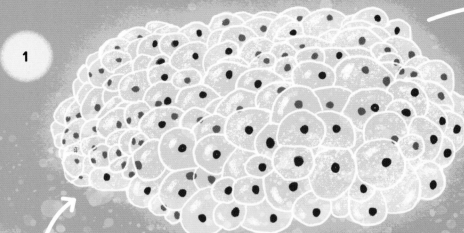

6

When the young frogs are fully grown, they can make babies of their own!

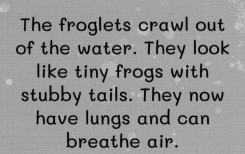

5

The froglets crawl out of the water. They look like tiny frogs with stubby tails. They now have lungs and can breathe air.

Tiny tadpoles hatch from the eggs. They have long tails that they use to swim. They take **oxygen** from the water using **gills**. Tadpoles eat pondweed.

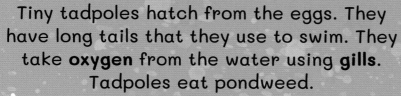

2

As the tadpoles grow larger, back legs appear. Their heads become more pointed in shape. Tadpoles start to eat other animals, as well as plants.

3

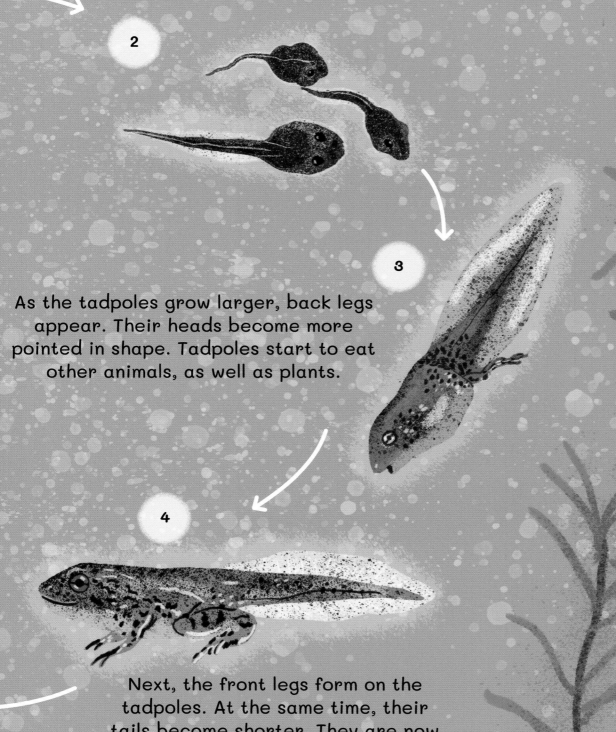

4

Next, the front legs form on the tadpoles. At the same time, their tails become shorter. They are now called froglets.

Make a Mini Wildlife Pond

Many animals make their homes in or around a pond. Attract tiny creatures to your backyard by making your own mini pond. You'll need a watertight container— the bigger, the better.

1

Find a good spot for your mini pond—some shade is best. Ask an adult to help you dig a hole to fit your container in.

2

When your container is in place, add a layer of stones and gravel at the bottom. Create different levels with larger rocks.

Old plastic container

Pond plants

Gravel

3 At one side, add logs and rocks to create "steps." This will help creatures get in and out of your pond.

4 Time to fill your pond! Natural rainwater is best for this. Leave some containers out in the rain, so you can use them to fill your mini pond.

5 Planting a few water plants will make your pond more natural and keep the water clear. You can buy these at garden stores.

6 If slimy green algae forms, scoop it out with a stick. It may take a while for creatures to visit your pond. Watch for bugs, dragonflies, and frogs!

African Grasslands

The great grasslands of Africa are home to many different animals.

Large **herds** of grass-eating animals roam the land, watched by hungry meat-eating **predators**. There are only two seasons here—a hot, dry season and a rainy season.

Oryx

Hyenas hunt in packs and also gobble up other predators' leftovers.

Lions live in groups called prides. These big cats are **carnivores**, which means that they only eat meat. They hunt zebra, wildebeest, antelope, or any other animal they can catch!

Giraffe

Giraffes are known for their long legs and neck. Their great height means that they can reach the juiciest leaves from the treetops.

Beautiful striped zebras are **herbivores**, meaning that they only eat plants, such as grass. Their stripes make it hard for predators to pick out a single zebra in the herd.

Warthogs are a type of wild pig. They push their snouts in the ground, snuffling up grasses and plant roots. Warthogs are surprisingly fast runners.

Warthog

Gentle Giants

Pandas are a type of bear. These large **mammals** live in chilly mountain forests in China. Giant pandas are very particular about the food they eat. They only eat the stems and leaves of the bamboo plant.

Bamboo

Bamboo is not very **nutritious**, so giant pandas have to eat a LOT of it. They eat for up to 16 hours a day, chomping up to 600 bamboo stems!

Despite their size, giant pandas are excellent tree climbers. They "hug" the tree trunk and use their sharp claws to grip onto the bark.

It can get very cold in the forest. Giant pandas have thick, waterproof fur that keeps them warm and dry during snowy winters.

A baby panda is called a cub. When it's born, the cub is small and pink, and has hardly any hair. It feeds on its mother's milk.

Red pandas are not related to giant pandas, although they both eat bamboo. These long-tailed mammals are about the same size as a cat.

In the Freezer

One of the coldest places on Earth is the freezing Arctic. Despite this, many creatures survive there. Some animals are white, so that they blend in with the ice and snow.

Arctic foxes have thick fur to keep them warm—even under their feet! When they sleep, they wrap their bushy tails around themselves like a blanket.

Walrus

Ringed seal

Walruses and seals have a layer of fat under their skin called blubber. This keeps out the cold when they dive for fish and other sea creatures.

Polar bears are the largest **predators** in the Arctic. They have an excellent sense of smell and can sniff out **prey** from far away. Polar bears hunt seals.

Whales are **marine mammals**. They spend all their lives at sea, but they come to the surface to breathe. Beluga whales are the only white whale. They feed on fish in the chilly Arctic Sea.

Scaly Reptiles

This group of animals has dry, tough skin that is covered in scales. Some **reptiles**, such as crocodiles and turtles, spend much of their life in the water. However, all reptiles breathe air.

Reptiles are cold-blooded, so they need to "bask," or warm themselves, in the sun. This is why most reptiles live in warm places. If it gets too hot, they find shade to cool down.

Crocodiles and alligators are the largest reptiles, known for their sharp teeth and strong jaws. They use their long, powerful tails to push themselves through lakes and rivers.

Texas tortoise

Unlike turtles, which live in water, tortoises live on land and eat plants. They have a bony shell on their back that protects them. Some tortoises can live to be 100 years old.

Most reptiles lay eggs. When the eggs hatch, reptile babies look like tiny versions of their parents. Many reptile babies have to look after themselves.

A crocodile's eyes and nostrils are on top of its snout. It can see and smell **prey** while its body is hidden below the surface.

Nile crocodile

The most common type of reptile are lizards. Most lizards have long tails and walk on four legs. They eat insects and other small creatures.

Snakes have long bodies and no legs. They can open their jaws very wide and swallow their prey whole. Some snakes are **venomous**, but most are harmless to humans.

Sand lizard

Milk snake

Deep-Sea Hunters

There are hundreds of different types of sharks, but the hammerhead may look the strangest! Its eyes are on both sides of its wide, flat head. This helps the hammerhead see to the sides.

Sharks have rows of sharp teeth that grow all the time. When a tooth wears down or falls out, a new tooth moves forward to take its place.

Eye

Sharks have amazing senses. They can detect tiny electric currents in the water. Hammerheads use these currents, along with their great sense of smell, to find food.

Hammerheads live in warm waters near the coast. They sweep their heads from side to side as they swim, scanning the ocean for **prey**.

Squid

Great hammerhead shark

Hammerheads eat sea creatures, such as fish, squid, crabs, and even other sharks! They use their wide heads to pin stingray to the ocean floor.

Stingray

Special Skills

Three-banded armadillo

Animals can go to great lengths to find a tasty meal—or to avoid becoming one! While some creatures are able to blend into the background, others can perform clever tricks.

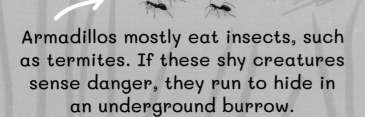

Armadillos mostly eat insects, such as termites. If these shy creatures sense danger, they run to hide in an underground burrow.

The armadillo is an unusual **mammal**. It has tough, scaly skin and hard, bony plates running from the tip of its nose to the end of its tail.

An animal's ability to blend into its surroundings is called camouflage. A tiger's stripes allow it to hide among plants, so it can sneak up on **prey**.

28

An armadillo's bony plates act like a shield. They protect the armadillo's soft body parts from attack by birds, foxes, and other **predators**.

If an armadillo is attacked, it rolls itself up into a tough, bony ball. This keeps even the most fearsome predator from taking a bite!

Bony plates

The chameleon's skin changes from green to brown, depending on how it feels. When it's angry, it turns stripy to warn off predators.

The **poisonous** porcupine fish is covered with sharp spines to put off predators. When threatened, it blows up its body like a spiky balloon!

Living Together

Meerkats are mammals known for standing upright on their two back legs. They live in large groups called mobs. Meerkats make their homes in large underground burrows in the deserts and grasslands of southern Africa.

Meerkats take turns to keep lookout while the others find food. If a meerkat spots a **predator**, it squeals a warning call to the rest of the mob.

Meerkats eat insects, **reptiles** and bird eggs, and even snakes and scorpions. When a meerkat eats a scorpion, it bites off the stinging tail first, so it doesn't get hurt.

Scorpion

Meerkat babies are called pups. All of the adults look after the pups, not just their parents. When an adult is babysitting, it can go the whole day without eating.

Meerkats depend on each other. When it's chilly, they snuggle together to keep warm. They will clean each other by getting rid of dirt and insects from their fur.

Life in the Desert

How do animals survive the dry heat of the desert? Some creatures burrow into the sand to escape from the burning sun. Others can go for a long time without food or water.

Fennec foxes have very large ears to help get rid of too much body heat. They also use them to hear insects and other small **prey**.

Fennec fox

Saharan silver ants are the world's fastest ants. They mostly stay in nests under the sand. They come out to find food for just 10 minutes a day. Their silvery hairs reflect the Sun's rays.

A camel can go for weeks without much food or water. It stores fat in its hump, which it uses for energy. Long eyelashes help keep the sand out of its eyes.

The **venomous** horned viper snake moves sideways very quickly across the desert. It buries itself in the sand and waits for birds and small **mammals** to wander by.

Jerboa

On the Move

Every year, some animals will go on a long and dangerous journey. They do this to search for fresh food, escape the winter, or to have babies. This journey is called **migration**.

Although they live on land, Christmas Island red crabs must have their babies in the sea. Every year, these crabs travel from their forest homes to the shore.

The red crabs' migration looks spectacular but is very dangerous. The crabs have to cross roads and avoid being eaten by other animals!

Wildebeest live in huge **herds** of around a million animals. They travel hundreds of miles across two African countries, searching for fresh grass and water.

Crabs are **invertebrates**. Instead of a skeleton inside their bodies, they are covered with a tough shell. Crabs keep shedding their shells as they grow.

The males dig burrows, where the females stay. After two weeks, the females leave the burrow and release their eggs into the sea. Then, the crabs walk home again!

Arctic terns have the longest animal migration. To escape from the coldest weather, they fly from the North Pole to the South Pole—and back again!

Big Bouncers

Kangaroos belong to a special group of mammals called marsupials. Marsupials keep partly developed babies in a pouch. Standing up to 2m (6ft 6in) tall, kangaroos are the largest marsupials. Most marsupials live in Australia.

A baby marsupial is called a joey. When it's born, the joey is tiny, blind, and hairless. It crawls through the mother's fur to a special pouch on her belly to grow.

Joey

The joey feeds on its mother's milk inside the pouch. A kangaroo joey is carried in the pouch until it's a year old.

Pouch

Kangaroos get around by jumping on their powerful back legs. They can leap a distance of nearly 10 m (32 ft) in a single bound.

The kangaroo's pouch is also useful for escaping **predators**. If the mother spots danger, the joey hides in the pouch. When the mother bounds away, the joey hitches a ride!

Koalas are another Australian marsupial.

These sleepy creatures spend most of their time snoozing in trees. A koala mother's muscles hold the pouch closed, so the koala joey doesn't fall out as she climbs.

Out in the Dark

Moth

When you're fast asleep, lots of creatures explore the quiet streets of towns and cities. Animals that are only active at night are called **nocturnal**. They are adapted to life in the darkness.

Nocturnal animals use the darkness to hunt or to hide from **predators**. Some might need to stay out of the heat of the day.

Foxes can be seen sniffing around streets at night. They often eat waste food that people have thrown away.

Owls are birds of **prey**. They hunt mice, frogs, and other small creatures. Their large eyes and excellent hearing help them find prey in the dark.

Bats are the only **mammals** that can truly fly. Bats squeak as they fly, and listen for the echoes, which helps them find moths to eat.

The European hedgehog can roll into a spiky ball to protect itself from nighttime hunters. It feeds on small **invertebrates**, such as slugs, snails, and insects.

Mouse

Collect Animal Footprints

Have you ever wondered which animals live near your home? Make an animal footprint trap, and find out if you have any backyard visitors!

1 Use an old baking sheet or tray for your footprint trap. Fill it with damp sand and pat to make a smooth surface. Check that your finger leaves a mark in the sand.

Fine sand

2 Put a little meaty pet food in a shallow dish or an old jar lid. Place the dish in the middle of your footprint trap.

PET FOOD

Fox

Cat

Rabbit

Find a quiet spot outside, and place the footprint trap carefully on the ground. Leave it overnight.

4

Next morning, check for footprints in the sand. Use the guide at the bottom of the page to help you find out which creatures visited!

Rather than pet food, try putting out seeds, lettuce leaves, and chopped unsalted nuts. Do you get different footprints?

Sunflower seeds

Bird

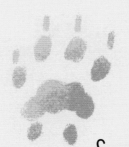

Squirrel

Mouse

Venom and Poison

Not all animals are cute and cuddly! **Venomous** animals inject harmful substances into their enemies by biting or stinging them. Other creatures are **poisonous**, which means that they will harm animals that eat or touch them.

Scorpions are **invertebrates**. They have eight legs and two large pincers, which they use to tear up **prey**. Their long tails are tipped with a venomous sting.

Scorpions can sense tiny movements on the ground or in the air. They lie still and wait for prey to come close—then they attack!

Deathstalker scorpion

The box jellyfish has long tentacles covered with stinging cells. It uses its deadly venom to catch its prey. A box jellyfish can even kill a human.

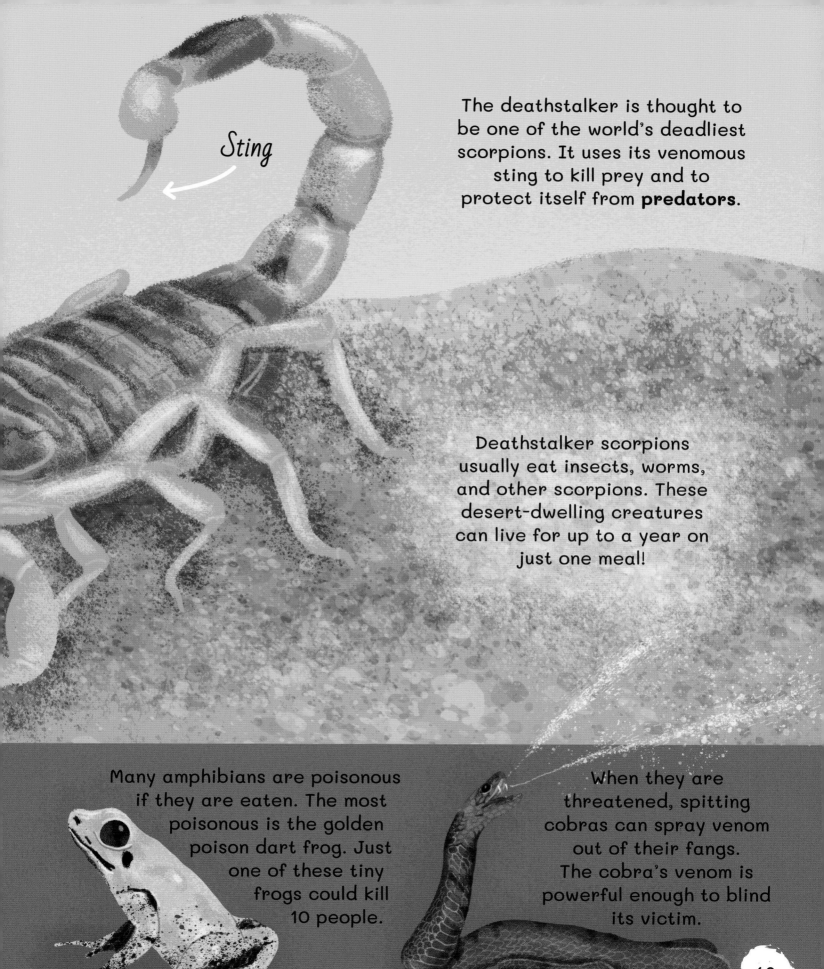

Sting

The deathstalker is thought to be one of the world's deadliest scorpions. It uses its venomous sting to kill prey and to protect itself from **predators**.

Deathstalker scorpions usually eat insects, worms, and other scorpions. These desert-dwelling creatures can live for up to a year on just one meal!

Many amphibians are poisonous if they are eaten. The most poisonous is the golden poison dart frog. Just one of these tiny frogs could kill 10 people.

When they are threatened, spitting cobras can spray venom out of their fangs. The cobra's venom is powerful enough to blind its victim.

Friendly Dolphins

Dolphins spend all their lives in the sea. Like all marine mammals, they must swim to the surface to breathe air. With their sleek bodies and powerful tails, dolphins are superfast swimmers.

Bottlenose dolphin

Dolphins live in groups called pods. The dolphins play together and look after each other. They work as a team to hunt fish and other sea creatures.

Dolphins call to each other with clicks and squeaks. Each dolphin makes its own special sound. If a dolphin calls for help, the rest of the pod will swim to find it.

Blowhole

A dolphin breathes through its "blowhole," which is a hole on the top of its head. When a dolphin surfaces, it sprays water out of its blowhole.

When a dolphin sleeps, half of its brain always stays awake. Because they have to swim up for air, dolphins cannot sleep deeply.

Animals in Danger

Some animals are **endangered**. This means that there are not many of them left in the wild.

Animals usually become endangered because of things that people do, such as hunting them or damaging their **habitats**.

Orangutan means "man of the forest." Orangutans belong to a group of **mammals** called great apes, which includes gorillas, chimpanzees—and us!

There are seven types of sea turtles, and all are in danger. Some turtles mistake plastic bags floating in the water for jellyfish and eat them.

Rhinoceroses are large **herbivores**. They live in Asia and Africa and are hunted for their horns. However, people are working hard to protect them.

Orangutans live in **rain forests** in Asia. They use their long arms to swing through the trees, looking for fruit to eat.

Because their forest homes are being cleared for farming, the number of orangutans has become smaller. However, lots of people are working to help orangutans.

Wildlife reserves have been set up to protect orangutans and other animals. Wildlife reserves are huge areas of land where hunting and the cutting down of trees are not allowed.

Years ago, people hunted humpback whales, and they nearly died out completely. Thankfully, since whale hunting was banned, the number of humpback whales has gone up. They are no longer endangered!

GLOSSARY

Amphibians   A group of animals that can live in water and on land, such as frogs, toads, and salamanders.

Carnivore   An animal that only eats meat.

Coral reef   A large underwater structure made up of lots of hard coral joined together.

Endangered   In danger of dying out.

Gills   The body part that lets underwater animals breathe by taking in oxygen from the water.

Habitat   The natural home of an animal or plant.

Herbivore   An animal that only eats plants.

Herd   A large group of animals that feeds on grass or other plants.

Invertebrate   An animal that has no bony skeleton inside its body.

Mammal   A type of animal that has hair and drinks its mother's milk.

Marine mammal   A mammal that lives some or all of its life in the sea.

Marsupials   A group of mammals that look after their babies in a pouch on their belly.

Metamorphosis   The process of an animal changing from one form to another as it grows into an adult.

Migration   A seasonal journey that an animal makes, usually in order to feed or breed.

Nocturnal   Active at night.

Nutritious   Contains substances that are important for the growth and development of animals.

Oxygen   A natural gas in the air that is necessary for all life on Earth.

Poisonous   Contains substances that are harmful when touched or eaten.

Predator   An animal that hunts and eats other animals.

Prey   An animal that is hunted and eaten by other animals.

Rain forest   A thick forest found in warm, wet areas of the world.

Reptile   A scaly creature that lays eggs and must warm itself in the sun.

Tropical   Describes areas of the world that are warm or hot all year round.

Venomous   Contains harmful substances that can be injected into another animal by biting or stinging.